Singapore

An Illustrated Journey for Young Explorers
Discover the Rich Geography, History, and Culture of Singapore

Visit our author page for more children's books
Amazon.com/author/88

By Nicole Damon

The Story of Singapore
From Fishing Village to Global Metropolis

Once upon a time, long before the skyscrapers and bustling streets, Singapore was a quiet little fishing village. Imagine small wooden boats bobbing in the water, fishermen casting their nets, and the gentle sound of waves lapping against the shore. This was the humble beginning of a place that would one day become a shining star on the world stage.

In the early 1800s, a British official named Sir Stamford Raffles saw the potential in this little island. He believed it was the perfect place for a trading post due to its strategic location at the tip of the Malay Peninsula, where the Indian Ocean meets the South China Sea. So, in 1819, he established a British trading colony in Singapore, and that's when things really started to change.

Traders from all over the world began to arrive, bringing with them a mix of cultures, languages, and customs. The sleepy fishing village quickly transformed into a bustling port city, alive with the sounds of merchants bargaining and ships coming and going. It was like a giant marketplace, with goods from every corner of the globe being bought and sold.

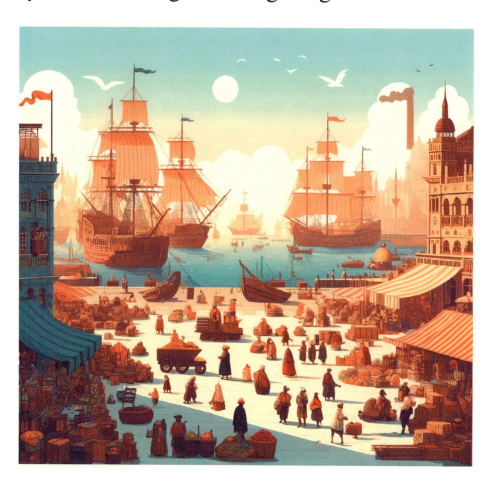

As time went on, Singapore continued to grow and change. It became a melting pot of cultures, with people from China, India, Malaysia, and many other countries making it their home. This diversity is one of Singapore's greatest treasures, creating a vibrant and colorful society.

But it wasn't always smooth sailing. Singapore faced many challenges along the way, including occupation during World War II and the struggle for independence. In 1965, after a brief union with Malaysia, Singapore became an independent nation. This was a turning point in its history.

Under the leadership of its first Prime Minister, Lee Kuan Yew, Singapore embarked on a remarkable journey of transformation. From improving housing and healthcare to developing a strong economy, the country worked hard to create a better future for its people.

Today, Singapore is known as a global metropolis, a shining example of progress and prosperity. It's a place where tradition and modernity blend seamlessly, where skyscrapers reach for the sky, and where the spirit of that little fishing village still lives on in the hearts of its people.

A Tapestry of Cultures: Celebrating Diversity

Welcome to the colorful world of Singapore, where every street and corner tells a story of diversity and harmony! Imagine a giant quilt made up of different pieces, each with its own unique pattern and color. That's what Singapore is like, a beautiful mosaic, with its rich tapestry of diverse cultures woven together to create a vibrant and harmonious society.

In Singapore, there are four main ethnic groups: Chinese, Malay, Indian, and Eurasian. Each group brings its own traditions, languages, and festivals, making Singapore a truly special place. Let's take a closer look at each of these cultures and see how they add to the magic of Singapore.

Chinese Influence

The Chinese community in Singapore, has introduced a wealth of customs and celebrations. Have you ever seen the incredible lion dance? It's a traditional Chinese performance featuring vibrant costumes and lively movements, believed to bring good luck and ward off bad spirits. It's an entertaining display that combines art, culture, and symbolism. During Chinese New Year, the streets of Singapore's Chinatown are filled with the lively sounds of drums and the colorful spectacle of lion dancers.

Malay Heritage

The Malays were among the original inhabitants of Singapore, and their culture is deeply rooted in the island's history. One of the most important festivals for the Malay community is Hari Raya Puasa, which signifies the end of Ramadan, the Islamic month of fasting. Families come together to enjoy delicious feasts and wear beautiful traditional clothing called baju kurung and baju melayu.

Indian Contributions

The Indian community in Singapore adds a splash of color and spice to the mix. One of their most dazzling festivals is Deepavali, also known as the Festival of Lights. During Deepavali, Little India, a vibrant neighborhood in Singapore, is decorated with bright lights and colorful rangoli, which are intricate patterns made on the ground with colored rice, sand, or flowers.

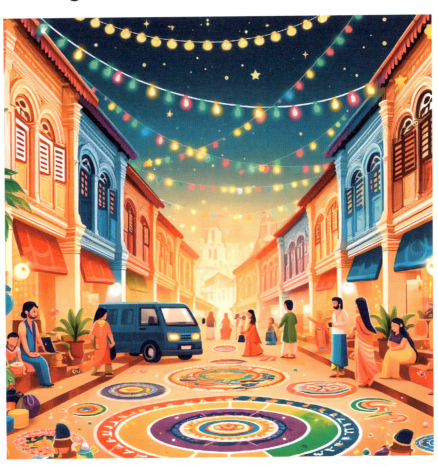

Eurasian Blend

Eurasians are people of mixed European and Asian descent, and they have a unique culture that is a blend of East and West. One of the most famous Eurasian dishes is the spicy and tangy Devil's Curry, which is usually made during festive occasions like Christmas.

But what's truly amazing about Singapore is not just the variety of cultures, but how everyone lives together in harmony. You'll find temples, mosques, churches, and synagogues all within walking distance of each other. And it's common to see people of different backgrounds celebrating each other's festivals and traditions.

A City of Green and Blue: Gardens and Parks

Welcome to the green heart of Singapore, where nature and city life blend together in perfect harmony! Singapore is often called a "City in a Garden," and it's easy to see why. Everywhere you look, there are trees, flowers, and parks, making the city feel like a big, beautiful garden.

One of the most amazing places in Singapore is Gardens by the Bay. Imagine giant tree-like structures called Supertrees, covered in plants and glowing with lights at night. It's like stepping into a futuristic forest! There's also the Flower Dome, a huge greenhouse filled with flowers from all around the world. And don't forget the Cloud Forest, where you can walk among misty mountain slopes and see the world's tallest indoor waterfall.

Another gem in Singapore's green crown is the Singapore Botanic Gardens. This UNESCO World Heritage site, with a history spanning over 160 years, is home to thousands of plant species. One of the highlights is the National Orchid Garden, which has the largest display of tropical orchids on the planet. It's like a rainbow of flowers, with every color you can imagine!

Architectural Wonders: Iconic Skylines

Get ready to be amazed by the stunning skyline of Singapore, where modern skyscrapers reach for the stars and architectural marvels tell the story of a city that's always looking to the future!

One of the most breathtaking sights in Singapore is the Marina Bay Sands. This incredible building looks like a giant ship floating in the sky, perched on top of three towering skyscrapers. At the top, there's an amazing infinity pool where you can swim and feel like you're on top of the world. And when the sun sets, the entire building lights up in a dazzling display that's sure to leave you in awe.

Another iconic landmark is the Esplanade, also known as the Durian because of its spiky exterior that resembles the tropical fruit. This building is a masterpiece of modern design and is home to a concert hall and theater where you can enjoy music, dance, and theater performances.

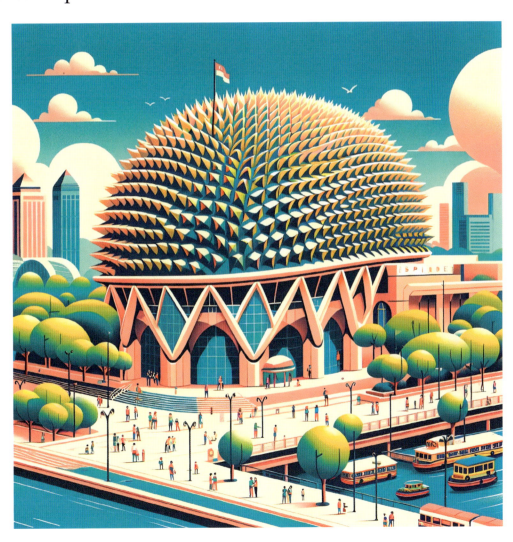

Heritage Buildings

But it's not just the modern buildings that make Singapore's architecture so special. The city is also filled with historic landmarks that tell the story of its rich past. One of the most famous heritage buildings is the Raffles Hotel, a grand colonial-style hotel that's like stepping back in time. It's named after Sir Stamford Raffles, the founder of modern Singapore, and has hosted many famous guests over the years. Don't forget to try the famous Singapore Sling cocktail in the hotel's Long Bar!

As you wander through the neighborhoods of Chinatown and Little India, you'll also discover colorful shophouses. These narrow, two- or three-story buildings are a unique blend of Chinese and European styles, with bright facades and intricate details. They're a beautiful reminder of the city's multicultural heritage.

A Taste of Singapore: Delicious Delights

Get ready to embark on a delicious journey through the flavors of Singapore! This city is a food lover's paradise, where every dish tells a story of the country's diverse culture and history.

One of the must-try dishes is Hainanese chicken rice. It's a simple but yummy dish of soft, gently cooked chicken served with tasty rice that's cooked in chicken broth. It's often accompanied by a tangy chili sauce and a refreshing ginger paste. This dish is so popular that it's considered one of Singapore's national dishes!

Next on the menu is laksa, a spicy noodle soup that's sure to warm your heart and tingle your taste buds. There are different versions of laksa, but one of the most famous is the Katong laksa, with its creamy coconut milk broth, rice noodles, and a mix of shrimp, fish cakes, and cockles. It's a perfect blend of spicy, savory, and slightly sweet flavors.

Don't forget to try satay, a delicious street food favorite. These are skewers of marinated meat, grilled to perfection over an open flame and served with a rich, peanut sauce. It's a tasty treat that's perfect for sharing with friends and family.

Best Places to See in Singapore
Marina Bay Sands

Get ready to be wowed by Marina Bay Sands, a true architectural wonder that has become the symbol of modern Singapore. This famous hotel and entertainment complex stands out with its three tall skyscrapers topped by a unique sky park that looks like a ship in the sky.

The rooftop infinity pool provides amazing views of the city's skyline, making it a must-see spot for anyone visiting Singapore. But that's not all – Marina Bay Sands also houses a luxurious shopping mall, a casino, and A diverse selection of dining options to delight your taste buds.

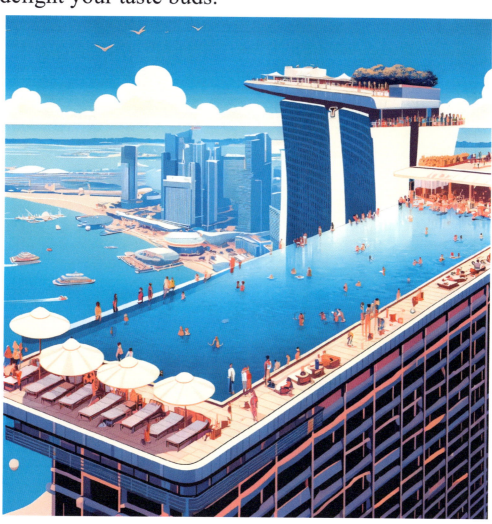

Merlion Park

No visit to Singapore is complete without a trip to Merlion Park, home to the famous Merlion statue. This legendary creature, featuring a lion's head and a fish's body, symbolizes Singapore's journey from a modest fishing village to a bustling metropolis. The statue stands tall, spouting water from its mouth, and offers a perfect backdrop for a memorable photo. Don't forget to admire the stunning views of Marina Bay while you're there!

Universal Studios Singapore

For a day filled with excitement and adventure, head to Universal Studios Singapore on Sentosa Island. This thrilling theme park features seven themed zones, each offering a variety of rides, performances, and attractions inspired by beloved movies and TV shows. Whether you're soaring on roller coasters, meeting your favorite characters, or experiencing the magic of movie-making, Universal Studios Singapore promises a fun-filled day for the whole family.

Sentosa Island

Speaking of Sentosa Island, this resort destination is a paradise for fun-seekers. With its sandy beaches, water parks, and attractions like the S.E.A. Aquarium and Adventure Cove Waterpark, Sentosa Island offers endless entertainment. Whether you want to relax by the beach, explore underwater worlds, or get your adrenaline pumping on thrilling rides, Sentosa has something for everyone.

Singapore Zoo and Night Safari

For animal lovers, the Singapore Zoo and Night Safari are must-visit destinations. The zoo is renowned for its open-concept enclosures, where you can see animals roaming in naturalistic habitats. From majestic elephants to playful orangutans, the zoo offers an up-close encounter with wildlife. As the sun sets, embark on a Night Safari, the world's first nocturnal wildlife park, where you can observe the nocturnal behavior of animals under the moonlit sky.

Chinatown

Welcome to Chinatown, a bustling neighborhood where the streets are lined with colorful shophouses and the air is filled with the delicious smells of street food! Here, you can explore vibrant markets, visit the beautiful Buddha Tooth Relic Temple, and taste some amazing dumplings and noodle dishes. Don't forget to pick up a souvenir or two, like a traditional Chinese lantern or a cute panda toy, to remember your adventure in this lively part of Singapore.

Little India

Next up is Little India, a lively area that's like stepping into a different world! The streets are bursting with the sounds of Bollywood music, the scent of spices, and the bright colors of saris and flower garlands. You can try some delicious Indian snacks, like samosas and dosas, or explore the stunning Sri Veeramakaliamman Temple. Little India is a feast for the senses and a place where you can experience the vibrant Indian culture right in the heart of Singapore.

Arab Street

Last but not least, let's wander down Arab Street, where the beautiful Sultan Mosque stands tall and the streets are filled with charming boutiques and cafes. This neighborhood is known for its stunning fabrics, Persian carpets, and aromatic perfumes. You can find beautiful souvenirs like intricate jewelry or colorful lanterns. Don't forget to try some mouthwatering Middle Eastern treats like baklava or falafel as you soak in the unique atmosphere of Arab Street.

Singapore's Future
Innovation and Sustainability

Singapore is not just a city of today, but a city of tomorrow, always looking forward with innovation and sustainability in mind. Imagine a future where buildings are covered in green plants, cars drive themselves, and technology makes life easier and safer.

Singapore is working hard to become a "Smart Nation," using cool technology to fix problems and make life better for everyone. But it's not all about technology; the city also aims to be a "City in Nature," creating more parks, protecting natural habitats, and developing eco-friendly towns.

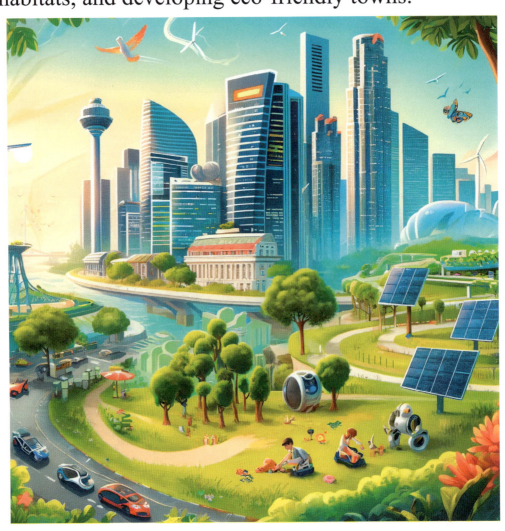

As we look to the future, let's be inspired by Singapore's vision. It's a reminder that with creativity, determination, and a commitment to sustainability, we can build a better world for generations to come. Singapore's future is about finding the perfect balance between progress and preservation, technology and nature, innovation and tradition. It's a bright future, not just for Singapore, but for the whole world.

Visit our author page for more children's books,
and remember to follow us for updates on new releases,
including illustrated storybooks, biographies,
fun-fact books, coloring books for kids, and more:

Amazon.com/author/88

Printed in Great Britain
by Amazon